HUMAN
CHARITIES
AND THEIR WORK

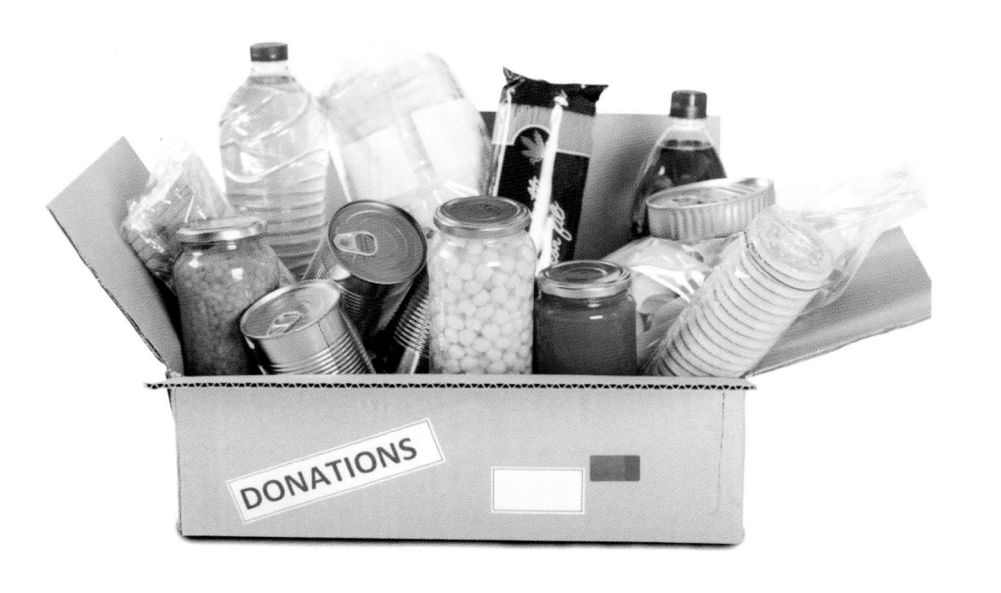

By
JOANNA BRUNDLE

ISBN: 978-1-78637-309-0

©2018
Book Life
King's Lynn
Norfolk PE30 4LS

Written by:
Joanna Brundle

Edited by:
Kirsty Holmes

Designed by:
Gareth Liddington

A catalogue record for this book
is available from the British Library.

CONTENTS

Words that look like **this** can be found in the glossary on page 24.

WHAT IS A CHARITY?

A charity is an **organisation** that supports people, animals or **causes** that need help. Charities need to raise money in order to do this work.

THESE PEOPLE ARE COLLECTING MONEY FOR A CHARITY.

People who work for a charity without being paid are called volunteers.

Collecting money for charities is known as fundraising.

SOME CHARITIES PROVIDE FOOD AND SHELTER FOR HOMELESS PEOPLE.

There are thousands of charities around the world. Each charity helps a different group in need. Charities do not make a **profit**.

People need food, clean water, clothing and shelter. Children need the chance to play and learn. Everyone needs healthcare and to be safe from danger.

Dirty water can cause serious illnesses.

SOME CHARITIES AROUND THE WORLD HELP TO PROVIDE CLEAN WATER.

WHAT DO PEOPLE NEED?

Without these things, people cannot live happy, healthy lives. They may become ill or die. Some people have to leave their homes to escape danger. They are called refugees.

A CHARITY HAS PROVIDED TENTS AND FOOD FOR THESE REFUGEES.

Some human charities help pay to build or run schools for children. Some charities teach their parents how to grow

A CHARITY PAYS FOR THIS SCHOOL, INCLUDING UNIFORMS AND FOOD.

HOW DO HUMAN CHARITIES HELP?

Some help people whose lives have been destroyed by natural disasters, such as flooding or earthquakes. Others help the elderly, or people who are being badly treated by someone.

Natural disasters destroy homes, shops, schools and hospitals.

SOME CHARITIES PROVIDE FOOD FOR PEOPLE WHO ARE STARVING.

HOW DO HUMAN CHARITIES RAISE MONEY?

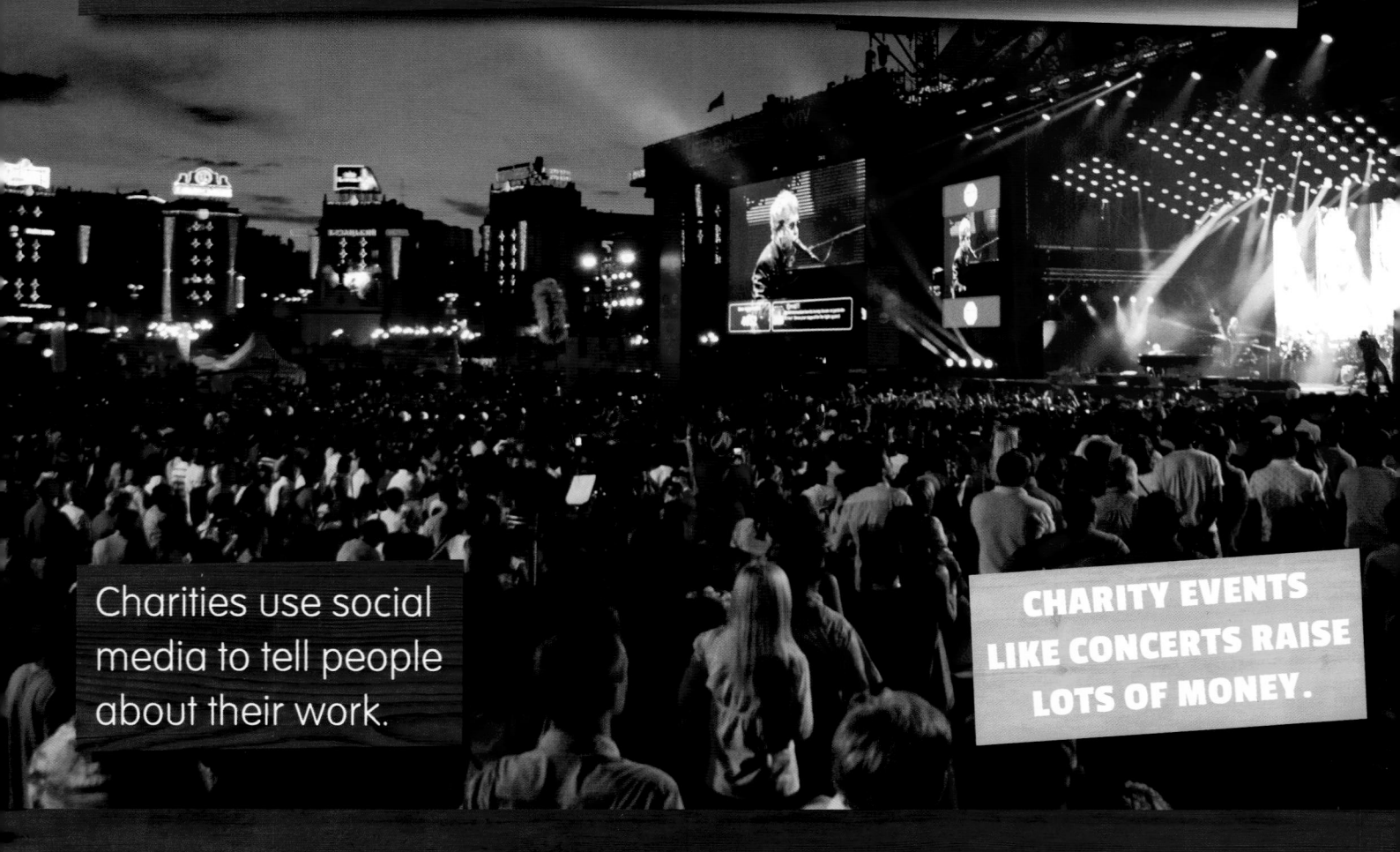

Charities use social media to tell people about their work.

CHARITY EVENTS LIKE CONCERTS RAISE LOTS OF MONEY.

Charities raise money by asking for **donations** on television and online. Emergency **appeals** on television and radio raise money quickly after natural disasters and war.

SPONSORING A CHILD CAN HELP THEM LEARN TO READ AND WRITE.

Some countries have a **national lottery** that gives help to charities.

Some human charities ask people to **sponsor** a child in need of help. The people make regular donations and receive letters and photographs from the child they are sponsoring.

HOW IS THE MONEY SPENT?

Some human charities provide life-saving equipment. Bites from an insect called a mosquito can cause malaria, a serious disease. Mosquito nets stop this happening.

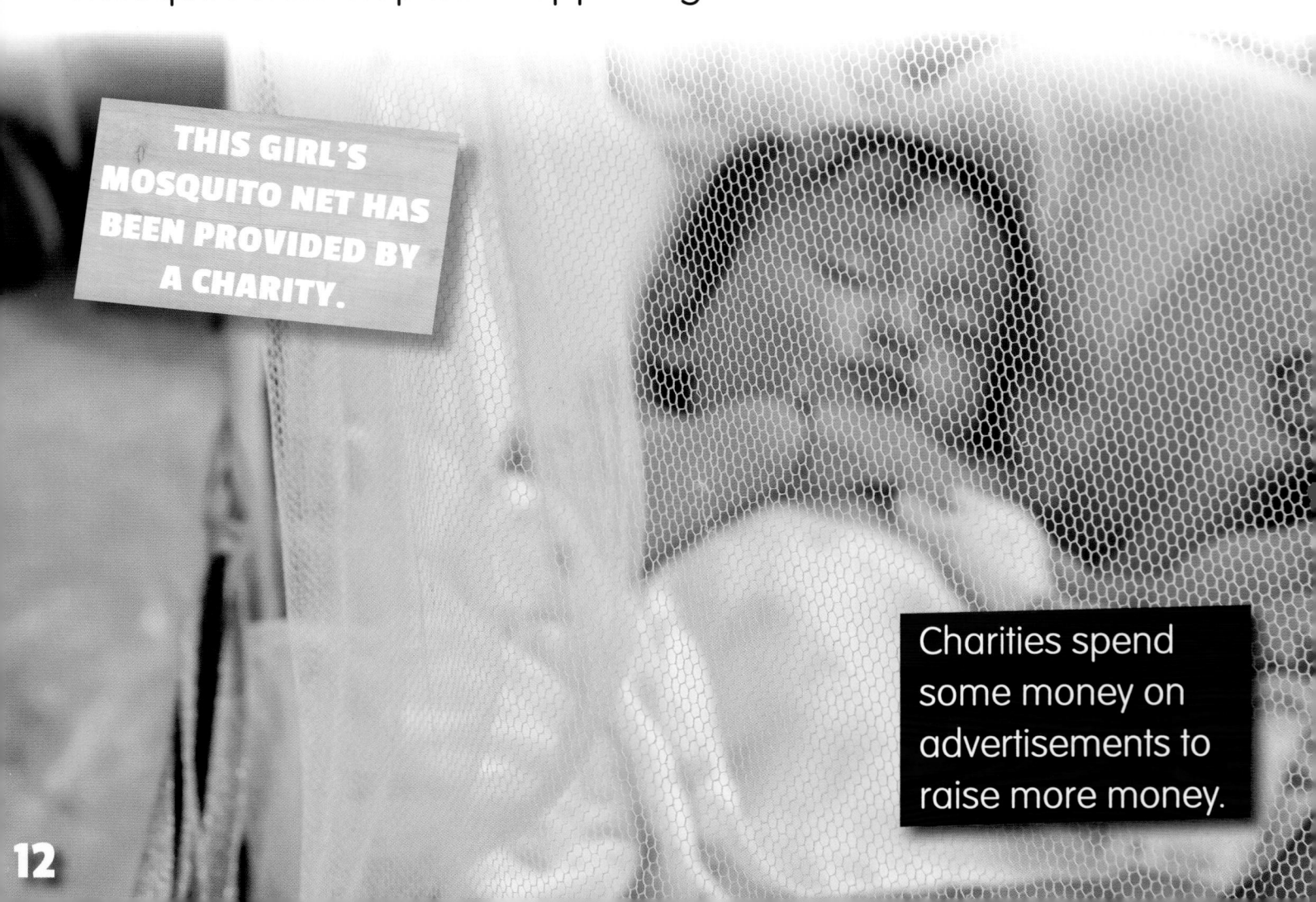

THIS GIRL'S MOSQUITO NET HAS BEEN PROVIDED BY A CHARITY.

Charities spend some money on advertisements to raise more money.

THESE CHARITY VOLUNTEERS ARE GIVING FOOD AND WATER TO REFUGEES.

Some spend money helping farmers in poor countries to grow more food. Others provide animals such as goats, which give meat, milk and manure for crops.

BARNARDO'S

Barnardo's slogan is 'Believe in Children'.

BARNARDO'S SUPPORTS YOUNG CARERS, WHO MIGHT BE LOOKING AFTER A FAMILY MEMBER.

Barnardo's is human charity in the UK that helps over 200,000 children every year. It cares for children living in fear or **poverty**.

Barnardo's organises care or **adoption** for children who have no family of their own. It also helps children who are being bullied or who are homeless.

BARNARDO'S HELPS YOUNG PEOPLE TO FIND WORK.

Save the Children is an **international** charity that works to save and improve the lives of children. It helps children affected by

AN EARTHQUAKE HAS DESTROYED THE VILLAGE WHERE THESE GIRLS LIVE.

This charity provides things people need, like blankets and soap.

SAVE THE CHILDREN

THE CHARITY PROVIDES VACCINATIONS AND MEDICINES THAT SAVE CHILDREN'S LIVES.

The charity began in 1919 and works in over 120 countries.

Save the Children also provides food and medicines. Kits containing paper and pencils help children carry on learning, even if their school has been destroyed.

Many children cannot go to school because they have to spend their days looking for clean water. Without it, these children and their families would die.

THESE CHILDREN HAVE TO WALK LONG DISTANCES TO FIND WATER.

THE WONDER OF WATER

A charity called UNICEF has helped millions of people by providing clean water. More children can now go to schools that have basic toilets and wash basins.

TOILETS AND WASH BASINS HELP TO STOP DISEASES FROM SPREADING.

19

HOW YOU CAN HELP

Find out as much as you can about problems that people face around the world. Tell your family and friends and ask them to donate.

EVEN SMALL DONATIONS CAN MAKE A BIG DIFFERENCE.

Look out for charity events and take part with your family.

Many charities have shops that raise money by selling things that people have donated. Why not donate clothes and toys that you

DONATIONS

DONATING TO A CHARITY SHOP IS A GREAT WAY TO HELP.

Maybe an adult in your family could help you collect some donations.

FUNDRAISING

A book sale at school is a good way to raise money.

A READ-A-THON WILL HELP YOU RAISE MONEY AND HAVE FUN!

Try organising a read-a-thon with your friends. Ask people to sponsor you for every book you read in a month.

A CAR-WASH
ALWAYS RAISES
LOTS OF MONEY.

Why not organise a car-wash at school? Ask all the parents
to pay to have their car cleaned by you, your friends and
your teachers.

GLOSSARY

adoption — providing a new family for a child who cannot be brought up by their natural parents

appeals — requests to the public for money or support

causes — issues that people are concerned about and want to support

donations — things that are given to a charity, especially money

international — involving two or more countries

national lottery — a game in which people choose numbers, buy a ticket and may win a large prize

organisation — a group of people, such as a club or charity, with a particular purpose

poverty — having very little or no money

profit — money made by a business after all its costs have been paid

sponsor — pay money to provide support

vaccinations — treatments designed to make someone immune to a certain disease

INDEX

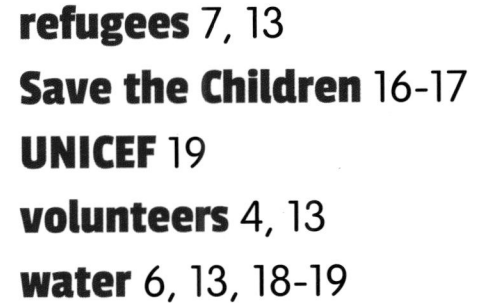